To Mr Brown

Tales of Dunlichity

from Alasdair MacQueen

desember 2001

Tales of Dunlichity
The Stories of Willie MacQueen

Edited by Charlie Fraser Larimer

Sigourney Press, Inc.

For a single copy of this book, please contact:
Sigourney Press, Inc.
1341 W. Fullerton Avenue, #244
Chicago, IL 60614
Web site: http://www.sigourneypress.com
E-mail: cfraser@sigourneypress.com

Book design and production by:
The Floating Gallery
331 West 57th Street, #465
New York, NY 10019
(212) 399-1961 www.thefloatinggallery.com

Charlie Fraser Larimer
Tales of Dunlichity

1. Author 2. Title 3. Literature 4. Short Stories 5. History
Library of Congress Catalog Card Number: 2001-131046
ISBN 0-9673863-2-2 Softcover

Dedicated to
Chrissie Patterson MacQueen

Willie's Wife and Childhood Friend

As told by
Willie MacQueen
to
Charlie Fraser Larimer &
Eric Fraser Larimer

Summer of 1996

Table of Contents

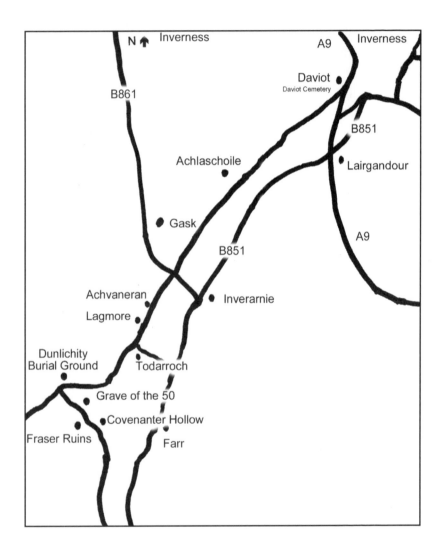

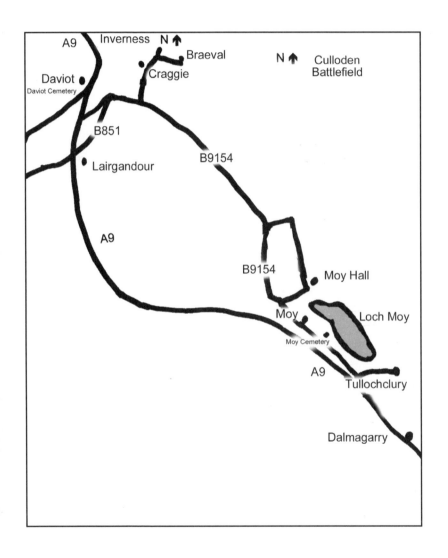

Willie MacQueen

Willie MacQueen at Lagmore Ruins

These ruins are the childhood home of Willie's great grandmother Catherine Smith and her brother Andrew Smith, Charlie Fraser Larimer's great great grandfather. Catherine and Andrew's parents were Alexander Smith and Catherine Rose, who are buried in Dunlichity Burial Ground.

Introduction

Several years ago on a trip to Scotland, I learned that a Scottish farmer named Andrew Smith lived near the crofts where some of my Scottish ancestors had lived, including my great great grandfather of the same name, Andrew Smith. My Andrew Smith had left Scotland and come to Canada in the 1830s amidst the Scottish clearances.

Hoping to find a family connection to the present-day Andrew Smith, we corresponded and traded genealogical lines. Although we have not found a direct connection, we both descended from Smiths that lived in a little village called Gask, south of Inverness in the parish of Daviot and Dunlichity area, so we are sure the connection is there.

These Smiths formerly went by the name of Gow, and are part of Clan Chattan, a confederation of clans initially drawn together for protection against some of their fierce neighbouring clans, particularly the MacDonalds of the Isles. Clan Chattan encompasses clans Mackintosh, MacGillivary, Davidson, MacPhail, Farquharson, MacBean, MacAndrews, MacDuff,

MacIntyre, MacLean, MacPherson, MacQueen, MacThomas, Shaw, and Smith/Gow. At the Battle of Culloden in 1746, located not far from where Willie's stories originate, Clan Chattan was positioned front and center in the unsuccessful charge against Lord Cumberland. "Touch not the cat but a glove" is their motto.

Shortly after exchanging letters with Andrew, I received the following letter:

Meadow Bank
Farr
Inverness
Scotland
25th May 1992

Mr. Charles Fraser Larimer
USA

Dear Charles,

I am the person who supplied Andrew Smith of Dunlichity with the information in respect of his forebears in this district & also the photo of Peter Smith. He lived with us in his declining years until his death. Andrew Smith's grandfather and my grandmother were brother and sister. The difference being Andrew's grandfather & father married late in life whereas my grandmother married in her 21st year to Hugh MacQueen of Ruthven, Tomatin, Inverness. I am now in my eightieth year.

Now I understand from your letters to Andrew that you are a solicitor [I'm not,] hense my reason for writing you is as follows. A granduncle of mine, Alexander MacQueen, emigrated to America in the 1860s. He died, I think, in the early first decade of this century. He was a bachelor and kept up correspondence with his brother all the years. The letters that came from America at the time of his death are now mostly lost, but I have two dated 1875 & 2nd March 1876. His address at that time was Clipper Mill, Watson Ville, Santa Cruz County, California.

Now I know that he was considered very wealthy and my grandfather, being his only brother, was heir to it. In those days, if anybody fell heir to a fortune in the New World, they had to go for it. My grandfather was all set to go, but my grandmother would not hear of it. Although their circumstances in these Highland Crofts left much to be desired, they did not go to America to claim the inheritance. Of course fantastic stories were coming to this country of how cheap life was in some parts of America at that time.

There was a couple by the name of MacQueen over here last summer, and after they went back they addressed a letter to MacQueen, Tomatin, Scotland. How I received it, I cannot tell, but they were looking for their ancestors who left these parts in 1830. I could not help them. But I told them the tale of my granduncle, but they never replied.

Since you are on that side of the water do you think there is any possibility of tracing that money? It must be considerable now if interest was added on all these years. If you could and did, doubtless you would share in the spoil.

More than likely the address in California I gave is no longer in existence, but his name will be somewhere and the money may have been swallowed up in legal work.

I hope this will not put you to too much trouble, because if there is no money, there will be no pay.

Yours sincerely,
William MacQueen

To date I am still unsuccessful in my search for the lost MacQueen fortune, although I have certainly tried to find it. My son and I even found the old Clipper Mill sawmill in California, mentioned in Willie's letter, which had been closed in the early 1880s. Throughout my search for the lost fortune I regularly wrote to Willie, giving him my progress updates.

In the summer of 1995 my son Eric and I traveled to Scotland, where I met Willie and Andrew in person for the first time. They and their wives were most cordial hosts, and all had tales of the region. After returning to the states, I sent Willie a tape recorder and asked him to tell me some more stories. These stories became the basis of this book.

Also, after further exchange of genealogical information, and after several years of correspondence between the two of us, Willie discovered that he and I are related as well – he is my mother's third cousin. I had always suspected some connection, in that my great great great grandmother was Catherine Rose, which was also the name of Willie's mother.

Willie was born February 4, 1913 on his father's farm at Dalmagarry Moy, about 12 miles south of Inverness. As he put it, he was born "in the U.S.A. (UpStairs in the Attic). All children of working people were born in their own homes in those days, as only the wealthy could afford to have them born in nursing homes." He recently celebrated his eighty-fourth birthday.

Although Alexander's fortune remains undiscovered, the treasures that Willie and I found were our friendship and these stories.

I would also like to add a special thank you to Willie's neighbour, Mrs. Morag Bulbrook, who supplied additional definitions of Dunlichity, and provided more information on the treacherous mass killings in the area. Another thank you to Sir James MacQueen Craig who provided additional stories of Lord Braxfield, the most notorious Queen's Counsel.

Charlie Fraser Larimer
March 1, 1997

Hello Charlie!

Hello Charlie!

You have my work cut out for me by sending me these tapes. I have tried a few people to see if they could help me to fill them up, including Andrew Smith and his wife, but what Andrew Smith said to me was "some hope, I told him all I knew." But, I'll try to give you a few more things about ourselves.

The MacQueens

Perhaps I should start with the MacQueens. Now the MacQueens were of Scandinavian origin and they settled around the Western Isles. They came across with the Vikings, but that was a long way back. I'll leave the Americans to guess when that happened. But the MacQueens came to this part of the world from Skye.

It is said that a daughter of the Lord of the Isles was engaged to marry a son of the Mackintosh of Mackintosh, Chief of the Clan Chattan. There was a contingent of people sent from Skye to see that she was well treated and MacQueens at the head of them. For this work, they were given the lands of Corrybrough Strath Dearn in the Tomatin area – you must have passed through it when you were across here on your holidays.

Those MacQueens were very numerous at one period, especially two centuries ago, and there were many of them spread up and down the Strath. There were, amongst them, quite well-to-do people that were sheriffs and there were army men and there were farmers. Some of them were on the East Indian companies, lately on the tea plantations. I couldn't tell you where they weren't. But apparently they were a sort of warlike race.

The Last Wolf in Scotland

The last wolf killed in Scotland was slain by a Donald MacQueen in 1743, three years before the Battle of Culloden. Now Donald MacQueen had a croft away down the Findhorn Valley about two miles from where my great grandfather and his forebears had a croft. It so happened that this wolf killed two children at a place called Tullochclury. That is a part of the farm in which I was brought up.

The Mackintosh of Mackintosh of that day, the Laird, summoned all his tenants and any able-bodied person that was able to go and search for the wolf. And they were ordered to be at Moy Hall at a certain time the following day.

Now Donald MacQueen was late in coming to Moy Hall, and the rest were waiting, and the Mackintosh was very angry when Donald MacQueen arrived. And the Mackintosh began to give Donald MacQueen a right set to. So MacQueen left the Mackintosh to say all he had to say, and then MacQueen took the wolf's head out from under his plaid and threw it at the Mackintosh's feet.

Willie MacQueen

It so happened that Donald MacQueen was taking a shortcut across the hills to Moy and he came on the wolf. I don't know what means he had to kill it; likely it was some old blunderbuss. But in any case, Donald MacQueen killed the wolf. So the story goes. And it's quite a true story, of course!

The Most Notorious Queen's Counsel

Now, I was saying to you that there were sheriffs and all the rest of them. One of the most notorious of them was Lord Braxfield, a Queen's Counsel. He was a high court judge. And his motto was, "Bring me the prisoners and I will find you the law."

Additional Stories Of Lord Braxfield
(Supplied by Sir James MacQueen Craig,
former British Ambassador to Saudi Arabia.)

Robert MacQueen, Lord Braxfield, lived from 1722–1799. He was born the son of John MacQueen of Braxfield, Lanarkshire and was educated at Lanark Grammar School and Edinburough University.

He qualified as an Advocate in 1744 and a Counsel for the Crown in the forfeitures after 1745. He developed a large practice, and was made Lord of the Session (judge) in 1776 and Lord Justice Clerk (senior judge) in 1778. He was called by Lord Cockborn "the

Judge Jeffreys of Scotland" – Judge Jeffrey (1648-1689) being notorious for his flagrant abuse of judicial authority.

Lord Braxfield presided over trials for sedition in the 1790s in Edinburough, and his judicial severity was roundly criticized in Parliament. The Dictionary of National Biography says he was "coarse and illiterate, had a hard head for both drinking and thinking, and a tyrannical will." He spoke in an accent and dialect of exaggerated Scotch."

Many stories about him still exist. When a man said to him, "All great men were reformers, even our Savior himself," Braxfield replied, "Muckle [much] he made o' that; he was hangit [hanged]."

On another occasion he said to a defendant, "Weel [well] Jamie, awhether ye're guilty or no, I dinnaker [don't care]. But whichever it be, ye'll be none the waur o' a hangir' [none the worse for a hanging] so hangit ye'll be."

The Promise of the Lost Fortune

Of course, the young of the last century, when the colonies were opened up, many, many, in large numbers, emigrated to New Zealand, to Australia and to America – to The New World, as they called it. And so the old people died off and the result was that they almost died out.

All that's left in these parts now are the family that I am of, and a few cousins. Of course, I regret that the paper pertaining to my uncle Alexander MacQueen who emigrated to America back around 1860 or earlier – I'm not sure how long – are lost. If we had those papers, perhaps we would be able to find out what happened to his fortune and whether it was great or small. But I know it was considerable. But I'll keep to my promise that if you find it and there's millions, I'll see to it that you get one million. Will that do?

Did I tell you why Alexander MacQueen left Scotland and went to America? He was a farmer, a crofter, and rabbits were eating the grain that he had stored.

Willie MacQueen

Now Alexander caught and killed several of those rabbits, and in that he did not own the land, he was accused of being a poacher for killing those rabbits. He was given the choice of leaving the area or having the rest of his family thrown off the land, which is why he emigrated to America.

Abraham Lincoln

You know, Charlie, I've just been reading the life of Abraham Lincoln, that great statesman that you had and President of the United States who was assassinated about the year 1865. I really think that he was the greatest person that America ever had. I don't think that there was anybody since that compared with him in any manner whatsoever.

Of course, a lot of them since then, they weren't very faithful to their marriage vows anyway. The man you have in the present day [Clinton], I think he's the poorest specimen that America ever put up. But, maybe perhaps he'll get wisdom yet.

The Battle of Harlaw

Of course, I should have told you that one of the earliest records we have of the MacQueens is when the Lord of the Isles sent an army to the Battle of Harlaw. The MacQueens fought under the Mackintosh of Mackintosh; that was in the year 1411. I don't know who they were fighting against, but the battle took place at Harlaw in Aberdeenshire and the Mackintosh of Mackintosh and the MacQueens were defeated. But they managed to regroup, and they attacked again. That place in Aberdeenshire is known to this present day as "Held Again."

Charlie's notes:
In one of the bloodiest battles on Scottish soil, the Battle of Harlaw was fought between the Highlanders and the Lowlanders. The Highlanders outnumbered the Lowlanders ten to one, but the Lowlanders wore armour and at the end of the day it was the Lowlanders that remained on the field.

William's Family

Perhaps I should have told you earlier about my family. There were eight of us – five sons and three daughters. There is only one daughter and myself left now. The first to pass away was a sister. She was a nurse in Glasgow and she took pneumonia and she died at the age of 21.

The next to die was my oldest sister. She developed cancer and she died at the age of 53. Her name was Marjorie. My sister who died in Glasgow was Catherine.

About a fortnight after my second sister died, my brother – my oldest brother, who was Deputy Chief Constable of Aberdeen City Police – came through to the funeral, and he had a coronary while through and he never went back. So, it was just a fortnight between that brother and sister, and he was 55 years of age. My other brothers died since then.

There was Charles – he died about a year ago. He was rolling wool all day and he went to bed and then complained that he couldn't get breath and he rose, but within an hour or two, he passed away.

Willie MacQueen

And another brother, who was only 71 – they were all younger than me – he was sitting reading the paper. And whatever he saw in the paper, he said to his wife, "Just listen to this." And he began to read it and then his voice stopped and she looked around, and he had passed away as suddenly as that.

My other brother, Andrew, he developed cancer in the bladder or the kidneys or some part. Anyway, he was only 64 years of age when he passed away. So that is pretty well our history.

White Hares and Hard Times

Of course we passed through very hard times in the 1930s. Very few people had money. But up in those hills where we lived, we could always catch white hares, if you know what white hares are – mountain hares. They're much bigger than rabbits – two or three times bigger than rabbits. And then we would always have meat.

We would kill our own sheep and then we would always have a barrel of salt herring so that, frugal and all that it was, we were better off than many towns-people, who were almost in dire starvation. Because back in 1930s, the most that anybody would get from the Social Securities in those days would be five shillings a week per household to keep the soul and body together. And there was great starvation in the country. So we lived through hard times. We lived right through the wars and things got better.

About 1936 there was a time that sheep and cattle improved in prices, and things weren't quite so bad as they were previously. But then the war came along and then everything was rationed – food, clothes. I don't suppose it was like that in America and you won't remember anyway. We had to look after the little we had; if not, you were very bad off.

So, those years passed and here we are now, within four years of the millennium. I don't know what you're thinking, but I hope that there will be greater days ahead of the nations of the earth in the next millennium than there have been in this one. At least in the last 100 years anyway, and there will be great prosperity and there shall be peace in all lands. For, we read in the Scriptures, I'm sure you read it yourself, that "men shall turn their swords into ploughshares and their spears into pruning hooks (Isaiah Chapter 2, V. 4)".

I think at times that this is what the nations of the earth are doing now and they don't know it. They are fulfilling that which is decreed in the divine decrees. What do you think yourself? Do you think so or not?

The Roses
and the Robinsons

Perhaps you would be interested to hear something
about my people, the Roses. They were along at Daviot
on the farm of Braevall, just a croft, for a period of 600
years. In those days, there were large families and, of
course, the Roses spread over the district. But the
Roses that I am of were buried in Daviot, not in
Dunlichity. Although there were Roses buried up
through the strath here, they were not the same Roses
as I am of, where I am related to you.

Now I had a grand aunt. She left Daviot with her
cousins Roses and she sailed for America about 1824,
before my grandfather was born in 1825. She met a
man, Robinson, on the boat that they were sailing,
who was also emigrating. She couldn't speak English
and he couldn't speak Gaelic. But, somehow or other,
they got very friendly. And sometime after reaching
America, I don't know how long, they kept in touch and
they eventually got married.

I don't know what number of family they had. I
suppose it would be considerable because everybody

had big families in those days. But I do know that she had two sons. One was a professor and I can't remember his first name. He was Professor Robinson and his brother was Dr. Charles Robinson. They came across here, my mother told me, in the year 1904 to see the old country. They were both very old men at that time. I think they were roundabout the age 70 mark.

The Smiths

You were asking me in your letter and you were telling me about your relations. Just wait a minute while I get a hold of your letter. The Smiths – your great great grandfather was Andrew Smith. Now he had brothers William and Finlay, and Alexander who married a Marjory Fraser, and Hugh, and sisters Isabel, who married Andrew Sutherland, and Catherine, who married John Calder.

Catherine Smith and John Calder had, that I know, four of a family; two sons and two daughters. Their daughter Catherine married Hugh Rose, who were my grandfather and my grandmother. I remember Catherine, my grandmother, but Hugh Rose was dead before I was born.

Now the other daughter, Isabel, she married a man, Andrew Sutherland. They had the Farm of Lairgandour. That is the land as you turn off the A9 on the Fort Augustus turn-off if you'll remember or not, but along there in Daviot. Now, Andrew Sutherland, he died in mid-time of his days. I think it was consumption – TB as they called it. They had no family.

Willie MacQueen

His widow carried on the farm for some time. She engaged a nephew. I'm not sure if it was a nephew of her late husband or a nephew of her own. But he turned out to be a complete failure and she had to give up the farm, which she did in the year 1888. Now my mother, who was born in 1877, she remembered Isabel very well. She also had a house in Inverness and my mother used to visit there as a young woman – young girl, perhaps, as you'd say. And of course, she remembered her grandmother very well, who was a sister of your great great grandfather.

Now, you speak of William. He had the farm of a place called Achlaschoile. If you can manage to say that, you can call yourself a Scotsman! Now, William was attending some services – church services in Inverness, as it was customary in those days in the month of January. It turned out to be very stormy weather and there were people trying to get him to stay for the night in Inverness, but he wouldn't hear of it. He said he could easily manage to get home because it was only a matter or eight or nine miles distance. But he set out for home and the storm increased in severity, so that he missed his home and he was found dead behind a dyke about a half a mile past his own home. It was very sad in any case.

Now Finlay, there were quite a number of his descendants around the district, and the name Finlay followed on. Now we know one Finlay Smith. He was a policeman down in the south of Scotland. He is now retired. And there were others belonging to him in the district. There was another family of the same race, but they were in the motorcar trade. They're retired now, of course. So, that is the way the Roses came about.

I should have told you that Finlay Smith, who was the retired policeman, is a first cousin of my wife's, so there's a connection away back in the very distant past. But although he is a cousin of my wife, my wife is not of the Smiths. Her mother was a Mackintosh and her father was a Patterson. So, that's the way it goes, you see?

My mother's youngest brother was Thomas Rose. He emigrated to Canada when he was 17 or 18, along with some cousins. He had various employments after he got out there and then he took up farming – I think in the Alberta area.

And I had another two aunts who emigrated to Canada. They were living in Winnipeg. One was a Sinclair and the other was an Allen. But the family, I think, moved out to Vancouver and I think the descendants of theirs are scattered throughout Canada and I think America. But where they are and what their names are, I just cannot tell you.

Dunlichity, Duin Leuth-Cheud: The Grave of the Fifty

I understand that my cousin Andrew Smith was showing you and your son around some historical places on his farm, Dunlichity Farm by the Dunlichity Burial Ground. I think Andrew showed you where The Grave of the Fifty is located in his fields. That is where the name of "Dunlichity" originates. It means the grave of the fifty. That's Gaelic, you see? If you want to learn Gaelic, you can make a start with that – "Dun Lichit," it's the grave of the fifty. [Dun, Duin = mound; Leuth-Cheud = half a hundred.]

Now what happened here was that cattle thieves came up from the Lochaber area (that is down the Fort William Argyleshire way), which was a common thing in the bad old days when free booters roamed the country and lived off it. It was almost a yearly event for the people from those hard climes to come up through those glens, there were no roads, of course, and go down into the flatlands of Nairnshire and just drive away the stock, especially cattle. I don't know if there were many sheep in those days or not. And there were quite a number of people driving them away.

These lowland cattle thieves reached Andrew's place in Dunlichity there in the evening of that day, and likely they were tired. I don't know what happened, but there were two lowlanders left to be on sentry to watch in case they were followed by the owners of the cattle. And during the night – they must've been all asleep, maybe they were drunk for all I could tell you. But the men of Nairnshire overtook them – surrounded them and killed 50 of them. The only ones that escaped were the two men that were supposed to be the sentries, so the story is told!

Dunlichity (Duin Leuth-Cheud), the Grave of the Fifty

Outline of the unmarked Grave of the Fifty

Charlie's Notes:

As would be expected for an event that occurred roughly 500 years ago, there are several different versions of the story of the mass killings, and similarly, there are alternate translations for the Gaelic word Dunlichity. Willie's definition of the word Dunlichity is far more interesting than the other interpretations I have found.

In a work published in 1791, the Reverend Mr. Alexander Gordon said that the word Dunlichity derives from Dun le Chatti, translated as the hill which bisects the territory of the Catti, where Catti comes from Clanchatti, or Clan Chattan.

The Reverend J. Macpherson, M.A., Ph.D., in a work published in 1952, specifically disagreed with the Clan Chattan connection, and said that Dunlichity

derives from the Gaelic words flichead, meaning mois-
ture, or fliuch, meaning wet. Dun is a hill or a fort, and
Dunlichity translates as "the hill of the wet place,"
which Macpherson felt was a good description of that
part of the parish.

Willie MacQueen's definition of Dunlichity is con-
sistent with other historical writings of the area.

There were other massacres that took place in the
Dunlichity area, including one at Tordarroch, next to
the childhood home of Willie MacQueen's wife Chrissie
Patterson MacQueen. In the early 1500s, Hector
Macintosh, the acting chief of the Mackintoshes, led a
raid on Dyke and Darnaway Castle, the property of the
Earl of Moray and, of course, Moray became quite
upset.

Moray then called upon his Mackintosh vassals to
meet with him in person to tell him where Hector was
hiding. The Mackintoshes who attended this meeting
were either unable or unwilling to disclose the location
of their chief. In response, Moray viciously hanged the
lot of them "over the balks of the house where the
court was held."

Another version of this story was that the Earl of
Moray, in an attempt to discredit Mary Queen of Scots,
sent out a false command by Mary ordering this band
of Mackintoshes to gather at Todarroach. Moray then
ordered the mass hanging, which he blamed on Mary.
However, the people of the area quickly saw through
this charade, and properly lay blame to the Earl of
Moray.

The story continued that after the Mackintoshes
were hung, Moray had their bodies thrown into a
mossy bog behind the barn at Tordarroch. For many

years thereafter, to the surprise and horror of those farming at Tordarroch, spurs and boots still containing leg bones would work their way to the surface when the ground was moist.

Covenanter Hollow

Now Andrew brought you along again to a big hollow in one of these fields, which is known as the Covenanter Hollow. I am sure that if you are acquainted with the history of Scotland, you would have read and heard of the Covenanters. These were the early Protestant men and women of Scotland who were driven around the country and hounded from pillar to post by the Ecclesiastics of those days, who were Episcopalians or Roman Catholics. They tried to stamp out the Protestant religion, you see.

Of course, in those days there were a lot of people in the district, but there were no churches. There were no buildings. There were no roads. But there was an excellent hollow for speaking in. If you went down into that hollow and started to shout, you could scarcely believe your ears to hear how the sound echoed. And it was an ideal place for the Covenanters to meet. It was a hollow that could keep at least a couple of thousand people with great comfort and they could hear without any hearing aids or any of the present day appliances for such purposes. But that's my story about that part.

Covenanter Hollow

Outline of unmarked Covenanter Hollow—Stones mark the base.

The Grooves in the Stone Church, Bonnie Prince Charlie and The Battle of Culloden

I don't know what else Andrew showed you. Of course, he had to show you where Bonnie Prince Charlie and his Jacobite soldiers were sharpening their swords before the Battle of Culloden, which was the last big battle on Scottish soil which took place in 1746. Culloden Moor is only about 15 miles from Dunlichity.

You see, in 1745, Bonnie Prince Charlie, hoping to reclaim the British Crown for his father (who would have been King James VIII of Scotland or III of England) landed in Scotland and quickly raised a group of supporters. These followers were called Jacobites, coming from the Latin name for James.

You see, Prince Charlie fought a battle of Preston Pans, just east of Edinburgh, which was a victory for the Jacobite Scots over General Cope of the English Hanoverians, who fought for King George. Then, rather than follow up his victory, Prince Charlie spent six weeks in Edinburgh dancing with the women, and only then he set off for London to claim the crown.

But his conquest held up about 130 miles from London, where he was surrounded at Derby Town in England and then forced to retreat to Scotland. The Jacobites then fought and won a battle at Falkirk, just west of Edinburgh. Then they moved further north up to the Inverness area, and then camped about Dunlichity there, so the story goes. And the stone church at Dunlichity Burial Ground was where they were sharpening their swords before the Battle of Culloden.

In any case, it was the Battle of Culloden where the English, commanded by the Duke of Cumberland, defeated his distant cousin Prince Charlie and his Jacobite followers. That Prince Charles – or as they called him, Bonnie Prince Charlie – turned out just to be a drunken rogue at the end of his days.

I may have told you some of these stories before, but you must forgive an old man whose memory isn't what it was 50 or 60 or 70 years ago. But I'll tell you a few more stories. I haven't got long to survive because you could hear from my voice that it's a bit rough. I'm not just putting it on, I'm telling you.

Andrew Smith shows the grooves in the church at the Dunlichity Burial Ground where the Jacobite followers of Bonnie Prince Charlie sharpened their swords before the ill-fated Battle of Culloden.

The Captain of the Five and MacCrimmon's Lament

Well, there's a story I forgot. We were talking a good bit about the clans, but I didn't tell you about the Captain of the Five.

There was a blacksmith that was at Moy during the 45 Rebellion, when Prince Charlie was North here during the last campaign between the Scots and the English government, which took place in 1745 and 1746.

The Mackintosh of Mackintosh, the Laird of Moy Hall, was away with the English Hanoverian government troops, who supported King George. But the Laird's wife, who was an ardent Jacobite, was on the side of Prince Charlie. So, there were twisters in those days too. You see, in that family they fished both sides of the river!

Prince Charlie came to Moy Hall and he was in that house, the Laird's house, when someone came to them and told them that Lord Loudon and some of the English government troops were advancing from

Inverness to capture the Prince Charlie. Now there were only about five men loyal to the Jacobite cause left. The rest of the men of Moy were all off with the Jacobite army or the Hanoverians, I don't know which – whatever side they chose to fight for.

The Laird's wife then called the old blacksmith, Donald Fraser, and there were only four other men. And she placed these four Highland men down the old roadway to intercept Lord Loudon and the English troops. There were no roads, of course, but where the Laird's wife expected Lord Loudon and his troops to come. And it was dark and the English soldiers were coming at night to make a surprise capture of Bonnie Prince Charlie.

When the Highland men heard the English soldiers coming, they started playing the bagpipes, well blowing the pipes, anyway, and firing muskets. And the Lord Loudon, with a company of 200 men, thought that the whole of the Highland Host was there at Moy, and the English troops turned and fled.

But one of the Hanoverian pipers with Lord Louden, MacCrimmon from Skye, was killed in the melee as Lord Loudon's troops rushed to get away from the Highland Host as they supposed. But there was nobody there but five men. A bagpipe tune was afterwards composed, called "MacCrimmon's Lament."

Of course, the Highland blacksmith was voted a hero for what he did, and his anvil was at the front door of Moy Hall up until about 1940. The chief that was there in my young days died. He died about 1938. The anvil is still around Moy Hall today.

But, you see, there were twisters in those days too – families that fought on both sides of that conflict. A lot of them who fought for Prince Charlie lost their estates or lost their lives. But the Mackintosh was sly enough. Of course, he had good folk on his side, as you shall come to hear in a few minutes.

Charlie's Notes:
There are several versions of the story of MacCrimmon's Lament, which honours Donald MacCrimmon, who was killed in the skirmish at the Rout of Moy in 1746 during the last Jacobite uprising. One version is that on the night before he died, following a premonition of his own death, MacCrimmon composed the sorrowful tune, and that his sister later penned the mournful verses.

MacCrimmon's Lament

O'er Coolin's face the night is creeping,
The banshee's wail is round us sweeping;
Blue eyes in Duin are dim with weeping,
Since thou art gone and ne'er returnest.

Chorus

No more, no more, no more returning;
In peace nor in war is he returning;
Till dawns the great day of doom and burning,
MacCrimmon is home no more returning.

The breeze of the bens is gently blowing;
The brooks in the glens are softly flowing;
Where boughs their darkest shades are
 throwing,
Birds mourn for thee who ne'er returnest.

Willie MacQueen

Chorus

Its dirges of woe the sea is sighing,
The boat under sail unmov'd is lying;
The voice of waves in sadness dying
Say, thou art away and ne'er returnest.

Chorus

We'll see no more MacCrimmon's returning
In peace nor in war is he returning
Till dawns the great day of woe and burning,
For him, there's no more returning.

The American War of Independence

Now, when the American War of Independence was being fought around 1776, the chief of the Mackintoshes was first and foremost to help with the American War of Independence – to keep it for the British, of course.

And you know, he mustered 500 clansmen. They were made up of Mackintoshes and MacQueens and McPhersons and MacBains and, of course, there were Smiths among them because they were on his estate. They went across to America, and I think that they had a pretty hard time of it on their voyage; I think there were pirates and all.

They were there under the command of Lord Cornwallis and the army opposing the Americans was mostly English. But Lord Cornwallis was defeated severely by the Americans, of course, and that finished the campaign.

Willie MacQueen

After the defeat, it is quite possible that many of those Highlanders remained in America, because they had no way of getting back to Scotland. That's the same thing that happened to the MacQueens who went to the Battle of Harlaw in Aberdeenshire with the Lord of the Isles, as I have told you earlier. When the Highlanders and the MacQueens were defeated, they just stayed on in the country where they were, and that is how there are a number of MacQueens at this present time who are to be found in Aberdeenshire.

Willie's First Wages — The Beating

Now, perhaps you would like to know how I earned my first wages. There were a lot of grouse in Scotland in those days, and there were a lot of gamekeepers and the Highland Lairds and all that.

At the age of 10, I was sent out to the beating. Now, I don't suppose you know what the beating is. The wealthy people, they had the shooting of the grouse and they would be in the butts, which were the dug-outs. They used to collect all the boys and unemployed folks who used to drive the grouse, maybe a mile or half mile, in a semicircle right onto the butts where the men with the guns hid.

So it was quite a great time; I was getting six shillings a day. That was in 1923 when I was 10. But, of course, when it came on to 1930, when I was 17, it was the time of the Great Depression. My wage wasn't reduced because I was at such an age. But those that started then were paid according to their age; you started at three shillings and sixpence and from there it moved up.

King George V at the Beating

I'm not sure if I told you this story before about my first year at the beating, and how I put King George V off the road!

I was some days out with an old horse that my father had, an old Clydesdale. I was able enough to lead the horse. This particular day, I was sent to Moy Hall with a load of grouse in the paniers – paniers are a saddle on a horse with a basket on either side.

I got down to the larder, which is a cool pantry where the grouse were stored until sold, and after unloading, I was told that I could go home. It was either the last drive of the day, or the second to last drive.

I got a hand from the kennel boy to get onto the horse's back because I was only 10, you see. Now, if I came off the horse's back, I couldn't get on again.

So, going up the road, who should be coming down the road but the King – King George V and all his contingents – on foot, four abreast on the narrow road. They were like the children of Israel coming up from the Land of Egypt. There were four of them in front. The King, the Mackintosh, and I don't know if it was

Willie MacQueen

Lord Lovat or the Duke of Atholl, were right in the front. Then there were gamekeepers, there were detectives, there were policemen, all there to see that nobody interfered with the King.

And I was sitting on this old horse's back – an 18-year-old Clydesdale. The road was only nine feet wide anyway and the horse and the paniers were the most part of six feet wide. The old horse didn't know the King from anybody else and he just kept plodding on and I put the whole lot of them off the road. And I kept going.

I never lived it down for many a day. Of course, it died out with the generation, but it was quite an experience. It was many a time I heard that I put the King off the road! Well, that's the way... of course, many things happened...

The Battle of Corunna

I had another relative, James Cameron – I should have told you – he was in the Peninsular War.

The English and the French fought this war over the Iberian Peninsula, which is off the coast of Spain and Portugal, and was the last English foothold in Europe in the early 1800s. That war was around 1812, and led to the eventual downfall of Napoleon.

James Cameron was in one of the battles in this war, called the Battle of Corunna. You would have heard of the Battle of Corunna in the history of Scotland. You'd have heard the poem,

> "Not a drum was heard,
> Not a funeral note in our course to the ramparts
> we hurried,
> Not a soldier discharged his farewell shot
> Over the grave of the hero we buried."

That was General Sir John Moore. That was the man who was the commander of the British Army, and he was killed.

Willie MacQueen

"We buried him darkly, at the dead of night,
The sods with our bayonets turning
and the struggling moonbeams misty light
and the lantern was dimly burning.

Few and short were the prayers we said.
As we spoke, not a word of sorrow,
but steadfastly gazed in the face of the dead and
bitterly thought of the morrow."

The Horse and
the River Findhorn

Now, I'll tell you another story – a true story. They're all true stories I'm telling you. I know I never made any up at all.

On the River Findhorn from Coignafearn to Cawdor, a distance of maybe, I don't know, maybe 50 miles, there was only one bridge. But when people wanted to cross that river in other spots, there were special places for crossing on horseback, you see.

And one spot was down my grandfather's way, where there was a horse. There were travelers – peddlers or packmen as they called them in those days – that were selling different goods. The farmer would give the peddler his horse, and the horse would carry the peddler across the river, and the peddler would then jump off the horse's back and turn the horse around and chase it back, and the horse would come back in through the river.

But this particular day, a packman came, stranger to the farmer. This packman apparently wasn't acquainted with the horse and hadn't been on a horse's back at all. The river was fairly wide at this point; well, I don't know, but it but 80 or 100 yards wide at the best part.

The packman had started across the river with the horse and had reached near the middle of the river, and the horse started going around in circles.

The packman didn't know what to do! He must have been a Roman Catholic, because he started calling to the Virgin Mary to save him.

The crofter, who was standing on the bank that he had left, shouted to the packman, "Never mind the Virgin Mary! Pull the other rein, man!" So, the packman finally got across the river, but the story lasted a long, long, long time.

The Beggar and the Beggar's Wife

Now, I'll tell you another story – true story, perhaps not in every detail or the way it was said, but it's the truth.

There were hawkers that used to come around this part. There was a large family of them. I'm talking about the early 1920s. Chrissie, my wife, and I remember them quite well. They used to come here and there, and go around begging and the man himself, he begged for himself. He wasn't bad for begging, but he would be asking "tobacco?" of anybody.

Now, this beggar man had camped along the roadside there on this special occasion. There was another man coming along the road in the morning and he knew that the beggar man was out. And, he knew he would be asking for a bit of tobacco. And sure enough, when the man came up to the beggar, the beggar asked the man for a bit of tobacco.

"Oh," said the man, "the very thing I was going to ask you for. I hadn't a smoke today" which was the truth, of course.

Willie MacQueen

"Oh" said the beggar, "You should never feel like that," and he pulled a tin out of his pocket. There were about twelve pieces of tobacco in it that his family and wife and him must have been mooching, begging around the strath in previous days. And there the beggar was with plenty of tobacco, yet still looking for more!

Now, I think it was the next day the beggar woman called on my grand aunt (where my son lives now), to peddle her wares. My grand aunt – Mary Smith was her name – she was busy baking girdle scones. Remember the girdle scones? Maybe you never saw them in America, but those used to be very good.

The beggar woman opened the door and walked in. There wasn't such a thing as knocking or ringing the bell, there were no bells anyway. And the beggar woman came in, and when she saw the girdle scones she said, "Oh, what would my family give to get a scone like that for the bairns [children]."

So my grand aunt wrapped half a dozen scones in a piece of paper and handed it to the beggar woman. But, of course this beggar woman was a real beggar. She had a little pail, a "flaggon" she called it, and asked, "I wonder, what about some milk for the flaggon because the bairns have nothing." The bairns were off mooching somewhere else, you see.

Oh, the beggar woman gets that, then she wanted a little meal – oatmeal. And then she gets that and then she wanted a few salt herring to spare. She was very pleased to get that. And then, she wanted a few potatoes. And then the beggar woman asked if she had a bit of salt meat in the barrel, which used to be a common thing in the Highland crofts. So, there was no end to her asking.

And of course, whenever she was done of asking, then she tried to sell something out of the basket she had. It could be needles or pins or thread or dishes, bowls or cups.

Of course, I should have told you that the bairns were out looking in any dumps to see if they could get old syrup tins. The beggar woman's husband Angie was a kind of tinsmith, and he used to put handles on them and go back around selling them to the people for pennies, you know? But of course, when Woolworth stores came to Inverness, that finished all that trade.

But back to the story – and, then the beggar woman was wanting, wanting, wanting and she said, "Oh, I was wanting to get a sheaf for my horse – haven't a thing for the horse."

"Oh," my aunt said, "see my brothers outside." She was keeping house to two brothers, you see, she was a spinster, old in years. So, the tinker was just outside the door, and back in she comes. And she says, "Oh, I wonder, would your brothers manage to give me a bit of tobacco for the man. He didn't have a smoke today!"

But of course, my grand aunt knew the story about the tobacco from yesterday, and finally lost her temper and she said to the beggar woman, "What else are you going to be asking? The more you get, the more you want!"

And then my grand aunt said to the beggar woman, "I see you're expecting another bairn." "Oh yes," said the beggar's wife. "I am indeed, but we have to fill our bellies with something."

The Pig

Now this is another true story – when they were building the railway at Tomatin, and they were building the
viaduct across the Findhorn River at Tomatin – that
would be back about 1890.

Now there were a big lot of navvies [workmen],
because everything had to be done by hand in those
days and there were no machines for doing anything.
But the navvies had to fend for themselves in the
camp.

There were boys going to school and one of them
was Donnie Noble, as we called him. I remember him
quite well.

His mother, who was a bit of a miser, told young
Donnie to go to the camp and ask the men if they
would buy a pig for their use. The price of it was told.
So they agreed, they would take the pig – it wasn't an
old pig.

But the week went past and there was no word of
the pig. And I think nearly another week went past. So
they went and watched for the boy who was going to
school one of the days. And when the navvies saw

Willie MacQueen

Donnie, they went after him and they asked him, "What about the pig that your mother was going to sell to us?"

"Oh," said the boy, "the pig got better!"

The Bankers

Regarding the boy and the pig, his people for generations were looked upon as the meanest in the district and were nicknamed "the bankers." "To make a penny by hook or by crook" — did you ever hear that phrase? — was their motto.

A ploughman was engaged, as was the custom in those days, for six months and was only paid at the end of the six months. If the ploughman left before then, he got no pay. They, "the bankers," engaged a man and, at the end of the six months, he made up a very long poem about them. Remember, this was 100 years ago or more. I just heard it rhymed when I was young and remember two verses:

(1)   The porridge that we get my boys
it is so awful thin,
if you put it on a sliding board
it would slide to Craggie Inn.*

* Craggie Inn was about 9 miles distant.

Willie MacQueen

(2)   Up at six in the morning
at the turning of the hay.**
You get a piece of barley bread
that would frighten the de'il [devil] away.

** Hay was turned by hand in those days.

Coming! Coming! Coming!

Now, there were no laws back in the old days. Anybody could sell anything; you didn't need permission to sell anything. I mean, if you were at the roadside you could sell whiskey, or sell your butter yourself.

But there was a woman at one of those places where wayfarers would get ample drink – whiskey. Oh, I don't suppose it would be distilled whiskey, it would be home distilled anyway.

But she used to go to church and she invariably fell sound asleep in church. And the minister of the parish found out something about her – when people would be in the bar calling for a drink, the woman would be shouting, "Coming! Coming!"

So that day she was sound asleep in church and the minister thought he would really rouse her. He stopped the sermon and he shouted out, "Two pints and a half gill!" And she shouted back, "Coming! Coming! Coming!"

A Penny's Worth of Broth
and Two Spoons

Well, Charlie, I'm just about running out of steam. For old age, I can't remember many stories more. I'll tell you one more and then I'm finished. And I hope you understand them all the way through.

There was, along Daviot or there abouts, a plough-man who was going to get married. He came to work in the district with a farmer, you see. And the usual run of things in those days – that was back in the last century – you would stay for six months and then move on to another farm.

But this one, he was a pretty good worker and I think he came from the islands. So he stayed on and the time was getting on. He was more than a year and a half with the place.

Of course, what really kept him in the district was that he had a girlfriend. So the time came when he decided he was going to get married.

The ploughman asked the farmer if he could get a day off, or a part of a day off. It was very hard in those days. They worked from six in the morning to six at night, six days of the week, no holidays at any time of the year. But he asked the farmer if he could get off.

"Oh yes," said the farmer, "you'll get off after ten o'clock." So, he had to meet the girl and they had to walk to Inverness, which was seven or eight miles distant, and they had to go to the registrar, you see. And they would have to buy a ring and they had other odds and ends to see to.

And then they thought they would go to the minister last. They thought that they would get some food at the minister's house, which was reasonable to expect. So they did all their other business first, and then they went to the manse, which was the home of the minister. The minister heard their tale, and he promised to do everything for them.

And then he began to apologize that he just couldn't give them anything to eat because the lady of the manse was having her afternoon nap, and she didn't like to be disturbed. And the maid was out doing the weekend shopping, so they just had to leave the manse with empty bellies.

There were no places they called restaurants in those days. Just anybody could stick a sign up in the window and say, "broth" or "mince." And the ploughman and his girlfriend went into this place where they usually sold mince and potatoes, which was done then because it was easy to cook. The ploughman hadn't got very much money anyway in those days. Nobody had. The ploughman and his girlfriend, they had less.

The woman selling the food came forward and she said, "Well, my young man, what would you like? We have broth today and we have potatoes and mince. Cabbage to go with it."

The young ploughman, he was never in such a business transaction in his life! And he was quite a bit shocked to think they got nothing to eat at the manse. He just pulled himself together and he called out, "A penny's worth of broth and two spoons! What do I care for expenses when my lover's with me!"

So that's the end of my stories. Now I hope this will work. I don't think I'll be able to fill any more tapes. I've tried everybody else, and Andrew Smith just says "Ho, ho." You know Andrew Smith yourself. He's quite willing to talk about cows and sheep and prices, but he won't put anything on the tape for me.

And there's no old folks in the district. There's only one old man and he's over ninety, and I couldn't make out what he's saying anyway. He's so feeble.

I'm the oldest person in the district next to him. The people of this district are nearly all in-comers, and they know nothing of the history of it, which is a great pity. I regret myself very much that I never did take more notice when I was young and wrote many an anecdote that I heard, because a lot of them were true – maybe a little exaggerated, but very good stories said by the fires of olden times. So, Charlie and Eric, I wish you well for time and eternity.

Andrew Smith's Story of the Buckshot on the Gravestone

Back in the early 1800s, grave robbers used to haunt many of the Scottish cemeteries late at night, gruesomely pulling the recently deceased out of coffins and selling the bodies to the medical school in Edinburgh, where the instructors would coldly and indifferently dissect the bodies during the anatomy classes. These grave robbers would occasionally strike at Dunlichity Burial Ground, and of course the people of the area, whose ancestors had once killed fifty cattle thieves during a night attack, were furious. They built a watchtower in the western corner of the cemetery where, after every new burial, several men of the Dunlichity area would keep watch over the burial ground, protecting the body of the soul recently laid to rest.

This watchtower proved to be successful in discouraging would-be grave robbers from the Dunlichity Burial Ground. But one night, the guard of the evening saw activity in the graveyard, pulled out his blunderbuss and fired away. He missed the grave robbers, who ran from the grounds, and severely damaged the back of one of the gravestones.

Andrew Smith pointing at the back of a gravestone damaged by buckshot, fired by a guard in the watchtower at a would-be grave robber.

Christine MacDonald Smith's Story of the Fraser Ruins

These old stone foundations that mark the Dunlichity lands had walls and roofs up until about 1900 or 1910, according to Andrew's grandmother. Frasers lived here, and they were very, very poor. Andrew's grandmother told stories of the families being so poor that the mothers would still be breastfeeding their children until they were about three years old or so, because they had such little food.

Willie MacQueen

Christine MacDonald Smith, wife of Andrew Smith, at the Fraser Ruins.